A Tune a Day
For VIOLA

A Third Book
for Viola Instruction
in Group, Public School Classes
or Individual Lessons

[*Provides training in ensemble playing when used with the Violin and Violoncello books*]

By

C. Paul Herfurth

BOOK THREE – ADVANCED

TEACHER'S MANUAL

A complete guide for teaching "A TUNE A DAY" for either Violin, Viola or 'Cello; containing piano accompaniments

A very convenient book for home practice

BOSTON MUSIC COMPANY

BMC11002

FOREWORD TO STUDENTS

POSITION

It is probably advisable at this time to briefly review the position of the viola and its relation to the left hand.

The viola should be held firmly on the left collar-bone by bringing the left shoulder well under the viola, thus giving the necessary support. The chin should rest well up on the chin-rest. In this position the viola should be held WITHOUT ANY SUPPORT whatsoever by the left hand.

Your teacher should decide whether or not it is necessary to use a pad for supporting the viola in order to avoid cramping the left shoulder.

THE LEFT HAND

In order to use the fingers of the left hand correctly, much attention and THOUGHT must be given to the proper position of this hand.

With the drawing of the left elbow well under the viola, the thumb should be placed fairly well under the neck so as to counteract the pressure of the fingers on the fingerboard. The knuckle joint at the base of the first finger should rest *very lightly* against the right side of the neck. This is modified at times and does not touch the neck. The thumb is best placed opposite and under the first finger. Thumb knuckle NOT BENT. In this position your hand has the necessary freedom to permit the proper use of the fingers, is also relaxed to shift into the different positions, and to use the vibrato as well as respond to any demand expected of the left hand.

INTONATION

At this point of progress it might be well to analyze the two most important factors that go to make up the art of viola playing, *i. e.*, intonation (playing in tune) and bow control (tone production).

As an aid to truer intonation it cannot be too strongly recommended that the student devote a part of his daily practice period to the technical exercises on pages 31 and 32.

They should be played slowly at first, gradually increasing the speed. Give special attention to the development of a keen sense of relative pitch in hearing the various intervals.

Develop the habit of listening more critically to your own playing.

IMPORTANT RULE

As an aid in judging the distance from one finger to another, FINGERS MUST BE HELD DOWN WHENEVER POSSIBLE.

TONE PRODUCTION

Unfortunately the average student's right hand and bow arm is frequently neglected in an effort to develop left hand finger technic. The folly of such a procedure is obvious when we stop to consider that the bow produces the tones which the left hand prepares. Left hand technic is of little value unless the bow arm is capable of bringing it out tonally in an artistic manner.

A PART OF THE DAILY PRACTICE PERIOD SHOULD BE DEVOTED TO BOWING PROBLEMS.

THE HEART OF THE VIOLA

The BOW, which is the heart of the viola, should be held rather firmly with the fingers, this firmness however should in no way interfere with the flexibility of the wrist.

The bow MUST ALWAYS be drawn in a perfectly straight line across the strings. In order to do this, the hand and wrist motion must be sideways in line with the bow, and not in an up and down direction. The back of the hand should always be flat.

Frequent use of a mirror is recommended to see if your bow is being drawn in a straight line. **TRY IT.**

A Tune a Day

Book III

CHAPTER I

A Short Review of the First Position

Use a forearm stroke with complete relaxation of the wrist and elbow. Upper arm must not move. Use upper third of bow. Allow the first finger to bear slightly upon the stick to keep the hair evenly upon the strings.

A valuable exercise for string transfers. Use forearm stroke as in above exercise. Keep the right arm in such a position that the bow will lie well over two strings at once, so that changing from one string to the other can be done by a wrist motion only. Play legato, no break in the tone when changing bows.

Two notes slurred on one string. Use whole bow, also upper half and lower half. Play legato.

Two notes slurred on different strings. Use middle half of bow. Hold the bow well over the two strings. Relax wrist.

A valuable exercise for intonation and use of four strings. Use a forearm stroke in single bows and two notes slurred. Hold fingers down in crossing strings.

*Hold fingers down

Fr. Wohlfarhrt, Op. 74, No. 5

5

A short study for the staccato stroke. Use upper third of bow. Be sure to use the same amount of bow for the two eight notes as for the quarter note. Accent slightly the quarter note. Relax wrist.

R. Hofmann, Op. 25, No. 15

6

A very important exercise for sliding the fingers a half step up or down. Do not raise the fingers when taking the half step. Slide it along the string in a rapid motion so that the slide will not be heard. Use whole bow.

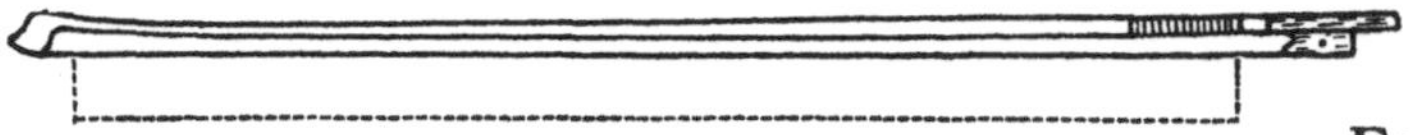

Fr. Wohlfahrt, Op. 45, No. 16

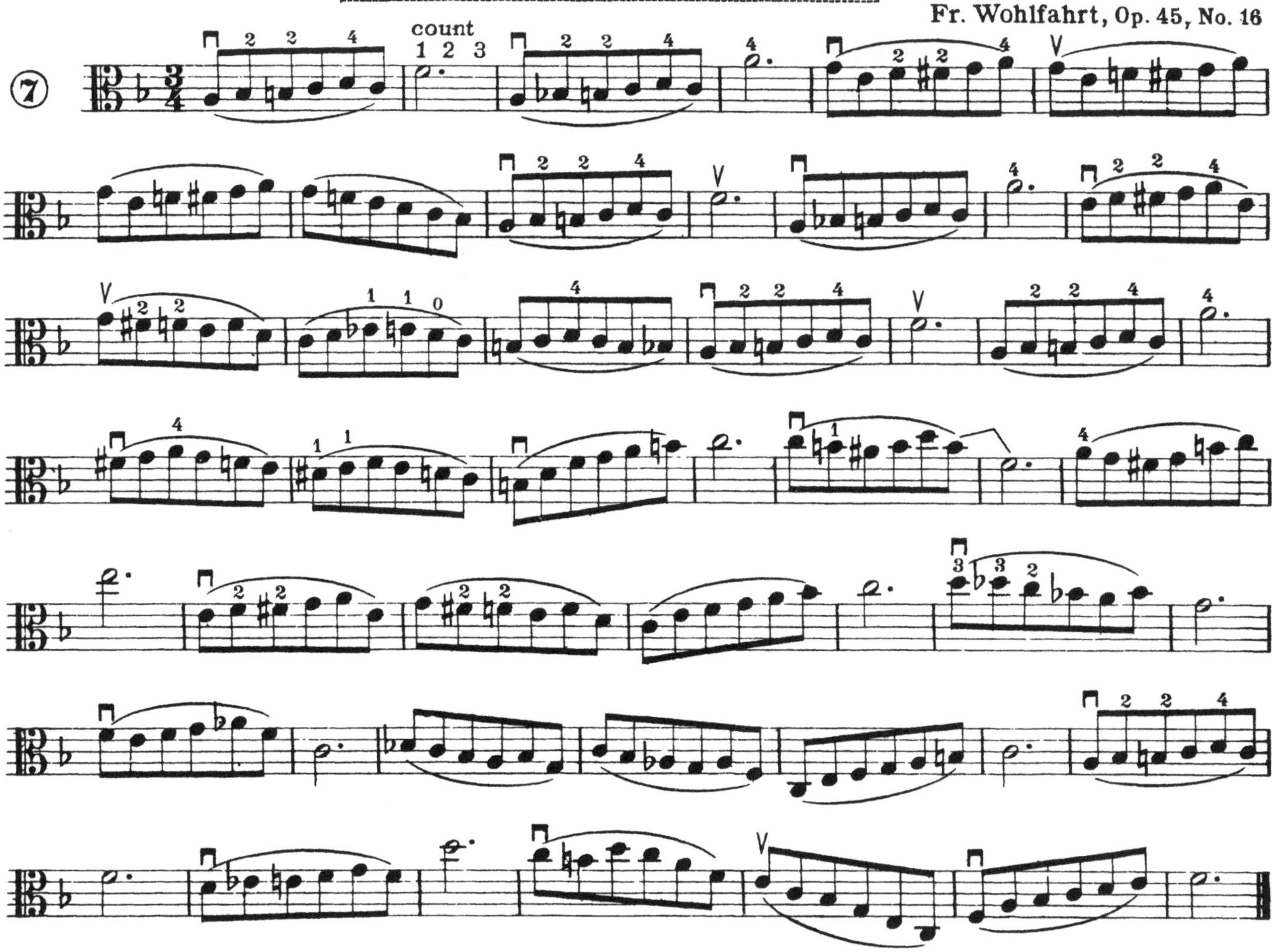
7
count
1 2 3

A study in triplets. Use the forearm stroke in both legato and detached style.

* Hold fingers down

D. Alard

8
count

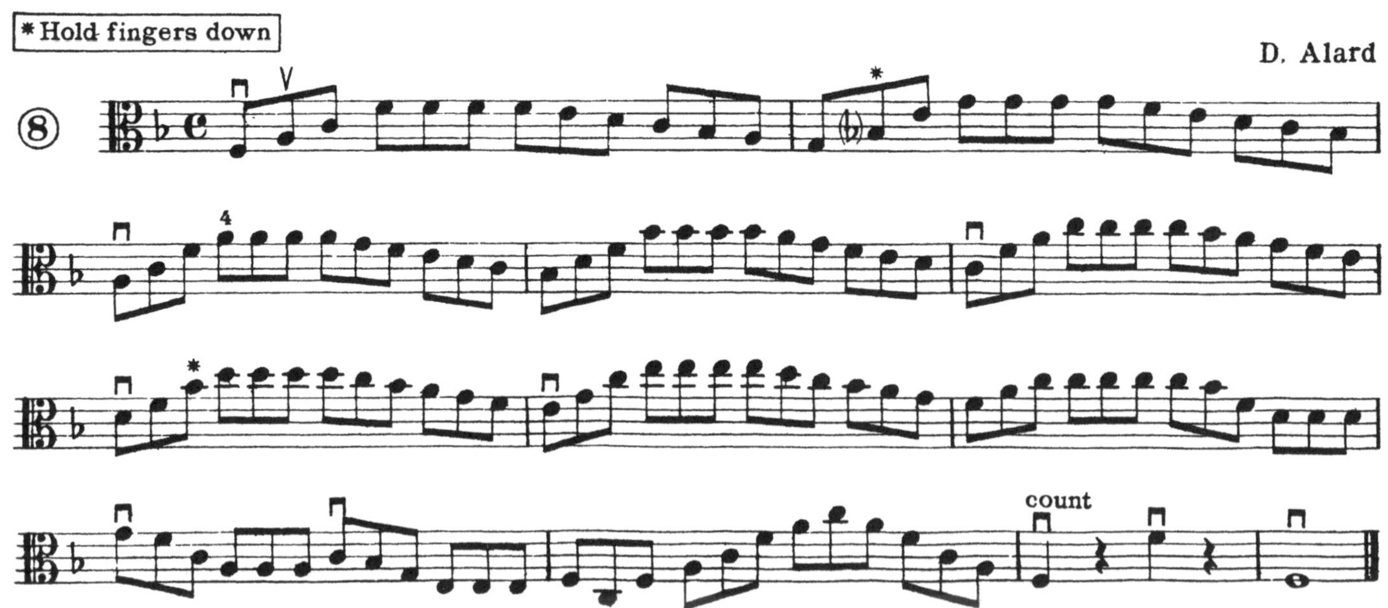

Étude

Use upper half of bow. Begin at the middle of the bow and play the eighth note to the tip at which point the sixteenth notes are to be played. On the next eighth note, return to middle bow and execute the sixteenth notes with short strokes at this part of the bow. Use a wrist stroke for the sixteenth notes.

M. Pt. M.

Fr. Wohlfahrt, Op. 45, No. 4

9

simile

A short study in rhythm. Use middle part of bow.

Étude

Fr. Wohlfahrt, Op. 74, No. 15

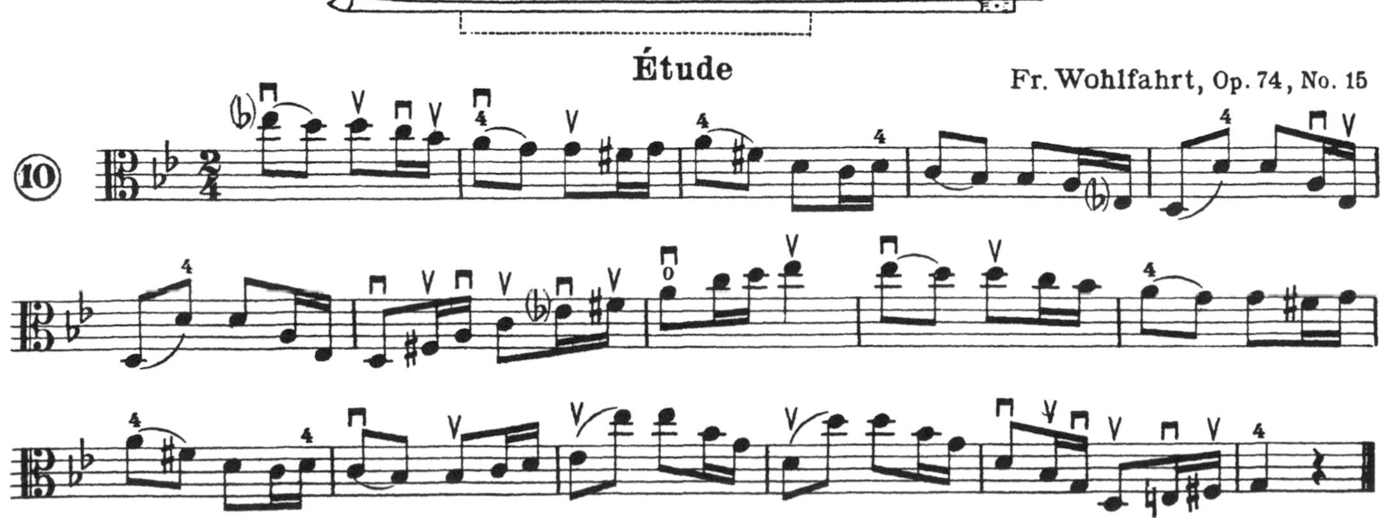

Duet Playing

Duet playing is a very valuable adjunct for the development of viola students and should therefore not be neglected. It is highly important in the furtherance of good sight reading, intonation and for freedom and precision of bowing.

Many self-conscious students will find duet and ensemble playing a great help in over-coming timidness while playing in public.

Be able to play either first or second part.

Viola I

F. Mazas, Op. 38, No. 2 Bk. 1

Viola II

F. Mazas, Op. 38, No. 2, Bk. 1

This is one of the most important and valuable bowings for orchestral playing. Use a wrist stroke in the upper part of the bow with a relaxed forearm. Hold the bow rather firmly upon the strings so as to stop the vibrations between notes.

A study in Syncopation. Be sure to master this valuable rhythm exercise. Do not accent unaccented notes. Play quite legato

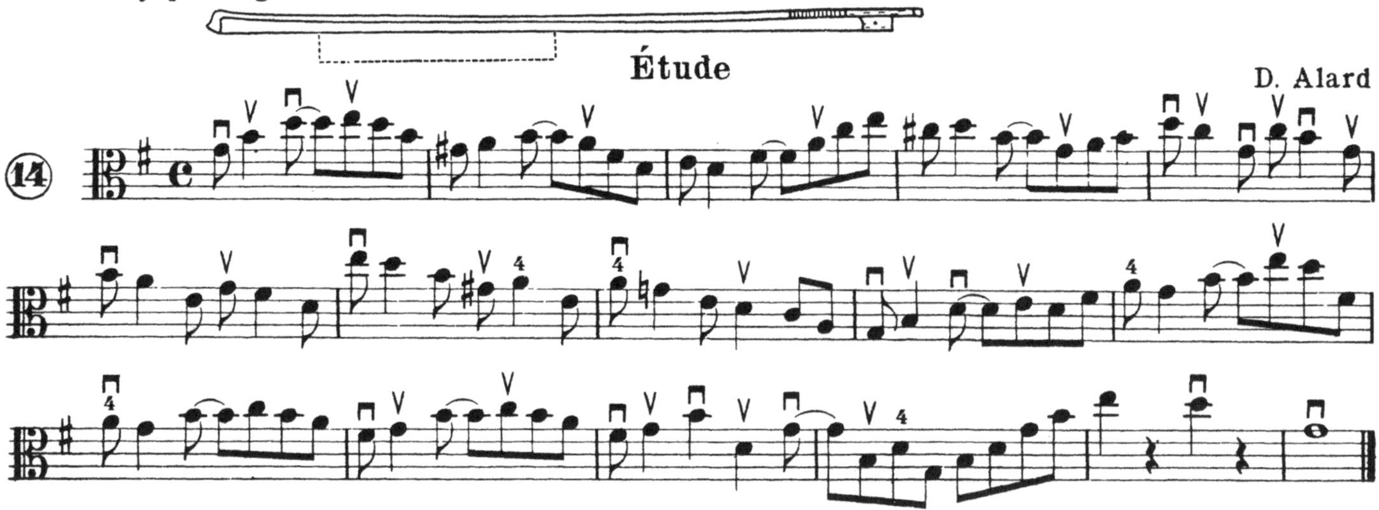

A study in octaves for intonation. Start with an up bow at the tip. Hold fingers down. Hold the right elbow fairly high.

CHAPTER II
Third Position

The word position refers to a particular part or section of the fingerboard used by the left hand fingers to produce certain notes without shifting.

There are some eleven positions in all, but for general use the first seven will cover the needs of the average violist.

Having studied the first position in books 1 and 2 we now take up the study of the second and third positions, but in reverse order. The third position, being used more frequently than the second, will be studied first.

The different positions are established by sliding the first finger diatonically (from one tone to another) up the fingerboard. Thus it will be seen that by moving the first finger on the A string from B up to C or C♯ we will be in the second position; and from C or C♯ up to D we will have established our hand in the third position.

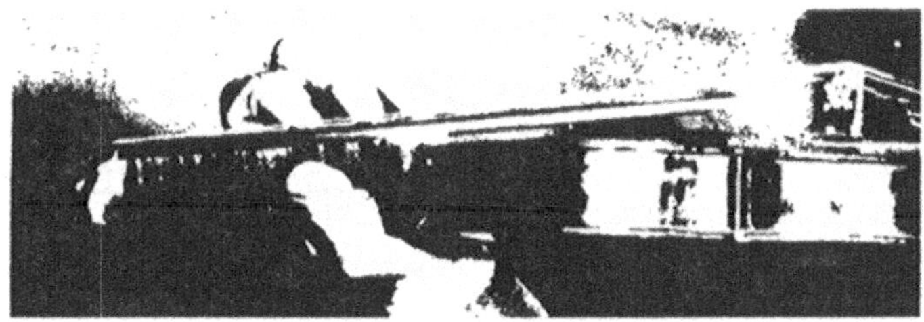

THIRD position from the left

THIRD position from the right

THE FIRST FINGER IN THE THIRD POSITION SOUNDS THE OCTAVE ABOVE THE NEXT LOWER STRING.

Important

THERE IS NO CHANGE IN THE RELATIVE POSITION OF THE LEFT HAND AND WRIST WHETHER PLAYING IN THE FIRST, SECOND OR THIRD POSITION.

The movement is entirely from the elbow.

It should be noted, the higher the position, the smaller will be the distance between finger placings.

On the D String

On the A String

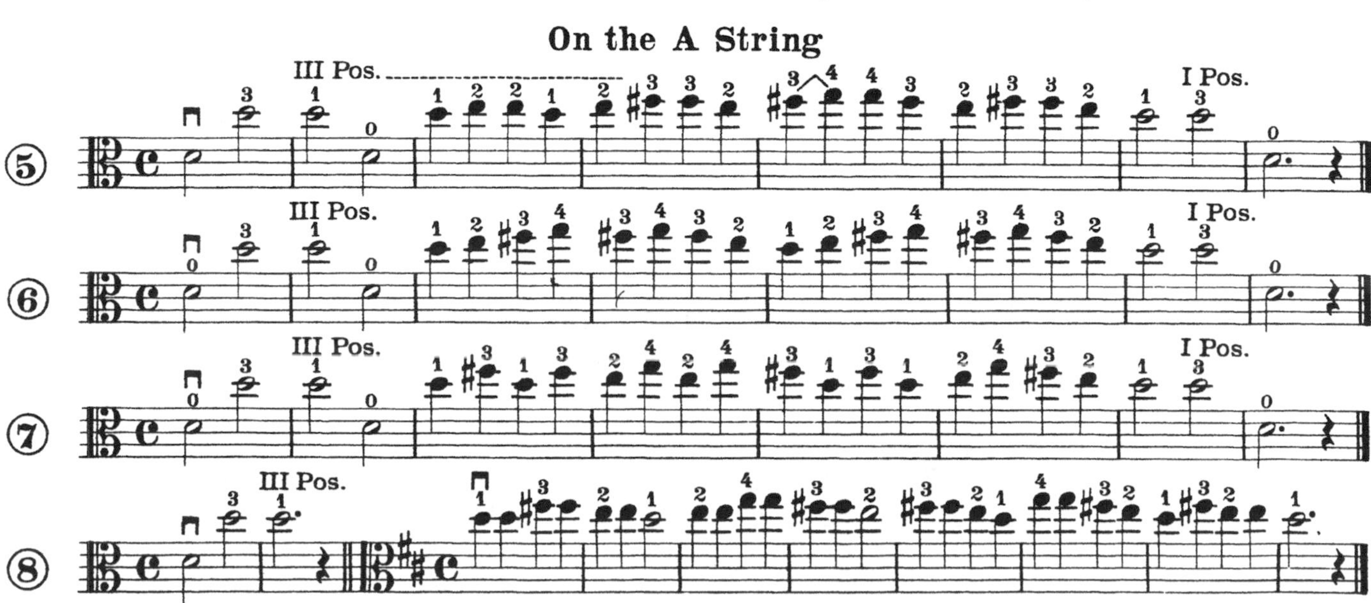

G Major scale and arpeggio in the third position

Play the above scale with different bowings as indicated.
Hold 1st finger on D and A strings.

Two short exercises for surity of fingering in the third position.

The First Noel

Divide the class, allowing half of the group to play the lower line in the first position while the other half plays the upper line in the third position to test intonation.

Old Melody

Third Position
On the G String

Third Position

On the C String

Key of F Major (One Flat–B♭)

CHAPTER III

Shifting To and From the Third Position while Playing Open Strings

When shifting, the hand must glide lightly without any griping of the neck. Be sure that the thumb is kept in the same relative position to the first finger while shifting.

G Major arpeggio in two octaves using first and third positions.

A most valuable exercise for changing positions, Use a forearm stroke single bows. Also varied bowings as follows, three slurred; three slurred three single; three single three slurred. Hold fingers down.

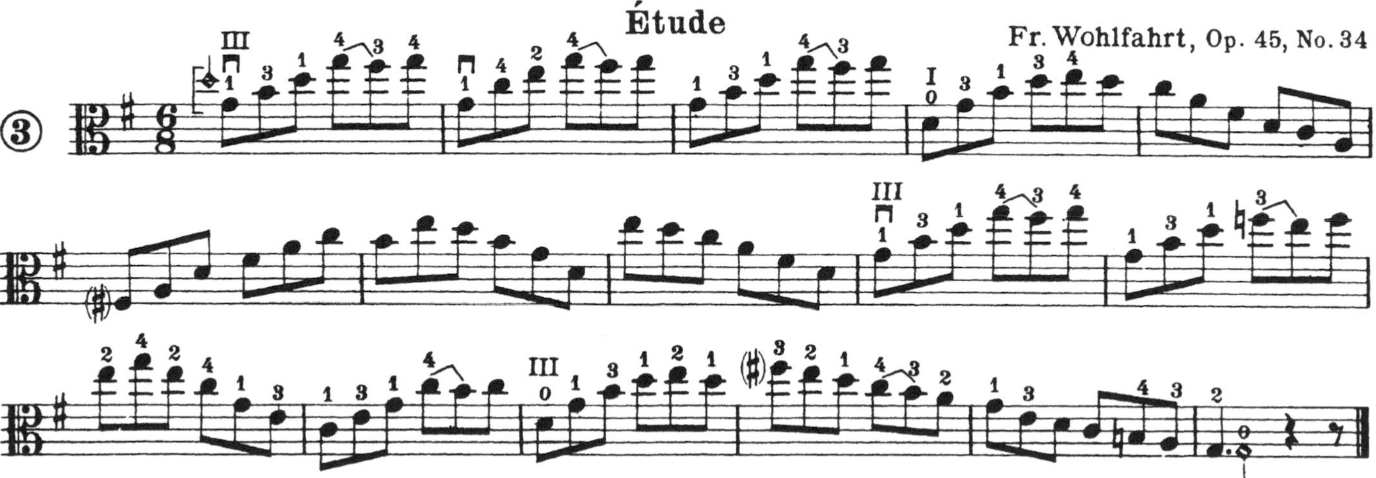

A good study for changing positions in legato playing. Use rather a full bow. Hold fingers down whenever possible. Place finger on two strings at once.

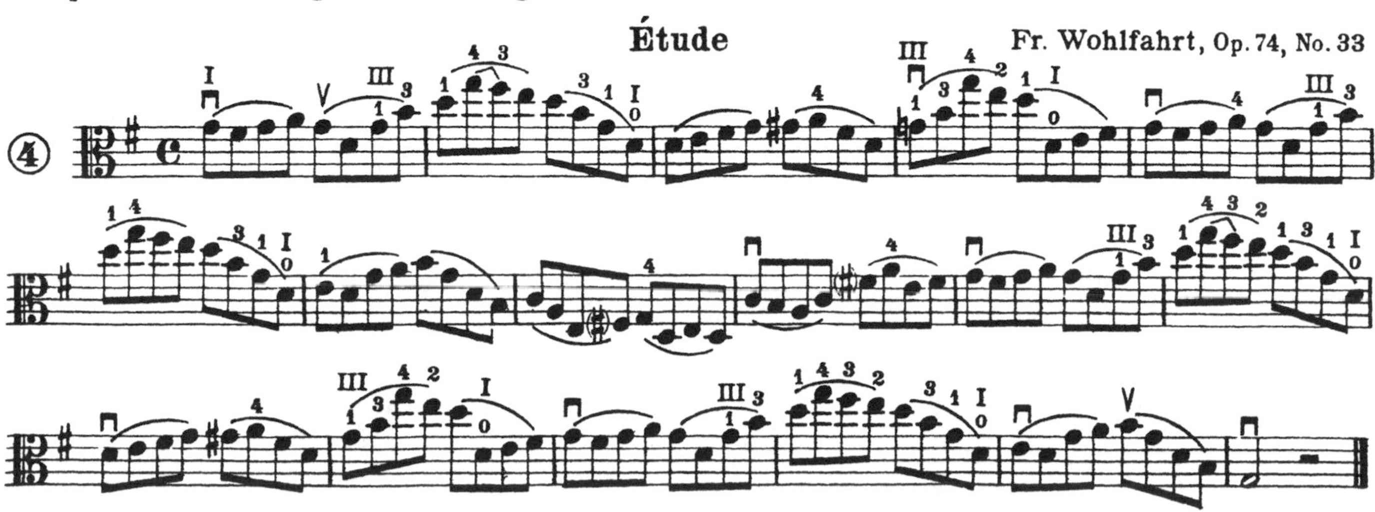

The two études on this page are of contrasting bowings. Use a rather full bow.

CHAPTER IV

Changing from First to Third Position with the Same Finger

In gliding from the first to the third position the hand, thumb and forearm must move together.

Allow the finger making the shift to slide up the fingerboard without taking it from the string. The pressure of the gliding finger however must be considerably lessened in making the shift. The thumb also must be completely relaxed.

Changing from a Higher to a Lower Position

In shifting from the third position down to the first the thumb and wrist must move in advance of the fingers. Move the thumb down the lower edge of the neck as far as possible to give support to the new position. As soon as the fingers reach the new position, the thumb should assume its normal position.

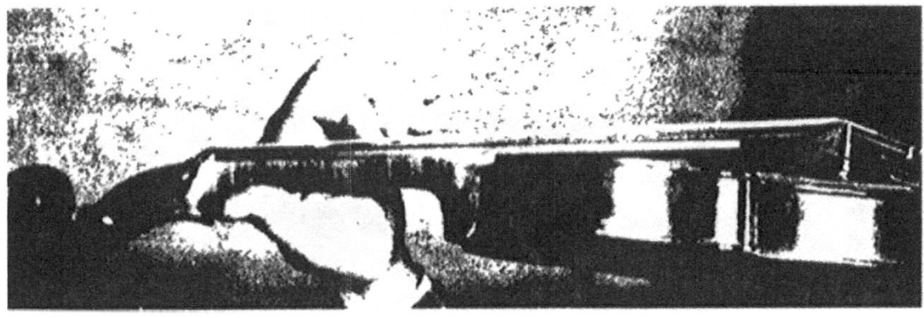

Showing position of THUMB in the descending shift from third to first positions.

These two exercises introduce changing positions portamento (gliding). Use a whole bow with freedom of the entire arm. Hold elbow rather high for string crossings. Full tone throughout.

CHAPTER V

Changing Positions with Two Different Fingers

The change of positions, using different fingers presents a new problem slightly more difficult than shifting with one finger.

THE SHIFT, EITHER UP OR DOWN IS ALWAYS MADE WITH THE FINGER COMING FROM, NEVER *WITH* THE FINGER GOING TO.

The instant the gliding finger reaches the new position, the new finger must be placed.

The small grace-notes show the position of the gliding finger, but should not be heard.

ALLOW THE HAND TO SHIFT FREELY IN AN UNCRAMPED POSITION.

Andante cantabile (slowly, in singing style) smoothness in connecting tones with changes of bow. Be sure to give notes full value before changing positions. Do not shift positions too slowly.

Étude

Andante cantabile

Fr. Wohlfahrt, Op. 45, No. 47

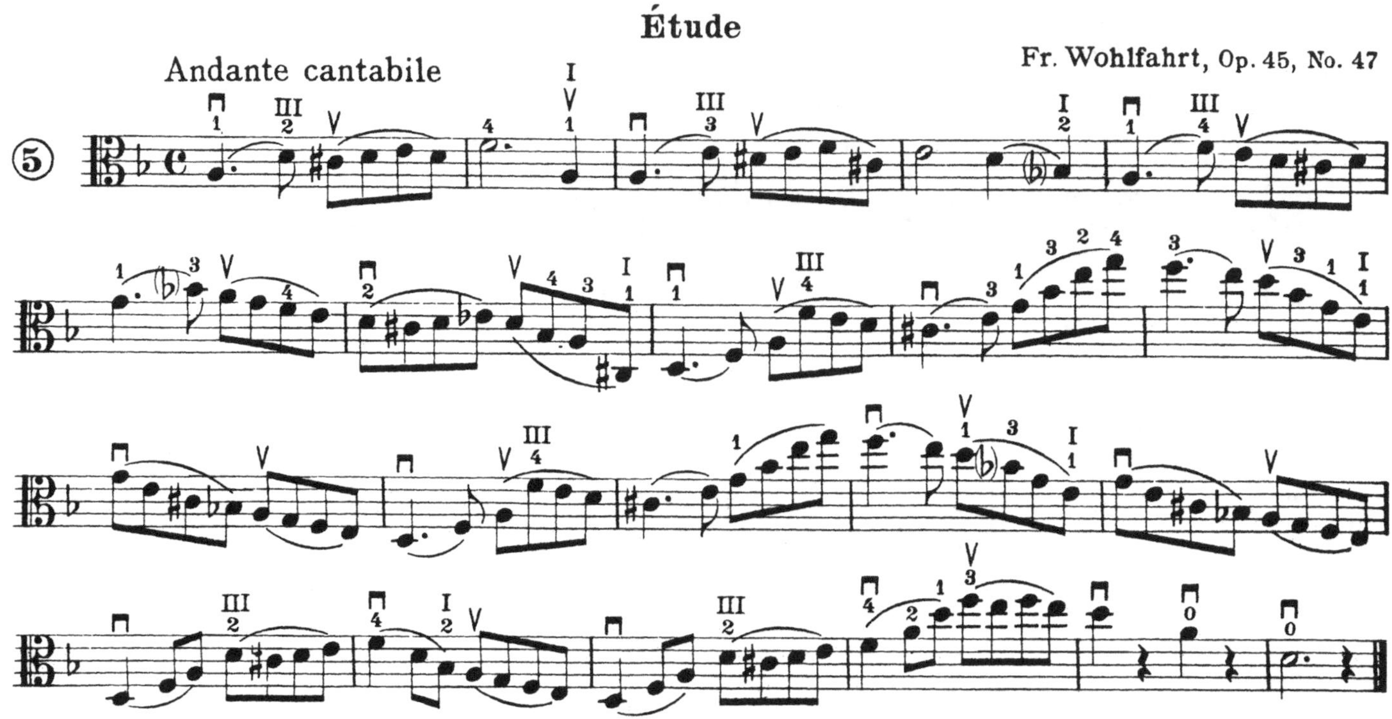

Broad bows and a full tone throughout.

Theme from Symphony No. 1

Allegro non troppo

Johannes Brahms

Graduation in tone. Play slowly with musical expression. Give full value to all notes.

Sweet and Low

Larghetto

Joseph Barnby

CHAPTER VI

Shifting Positions

(As in Scales)

Changing positions as used in scale passages is by far the most difficult to execute and should be practiced diligently.

Due to a difference of opinion as to how this shift should be made, any reference as to its execution seems to have been omitted in most instruction books.

The following examples show the two different methods of execution for this shift. Your teacher will instruct you as to which method to use.

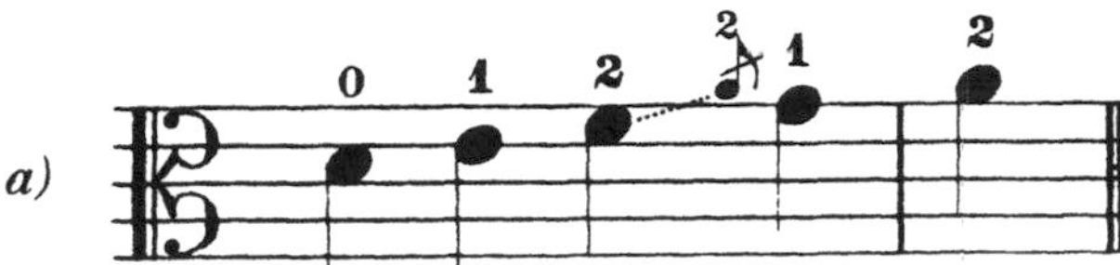

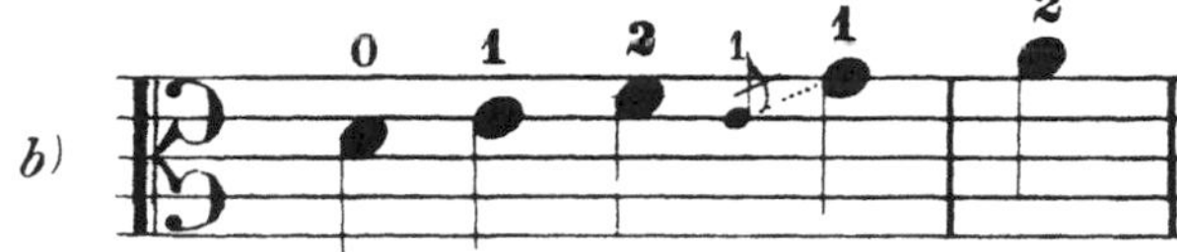

Example *a)* gives a better picture as to how to prepare for this shift, although in actual playing it sounds as follows:

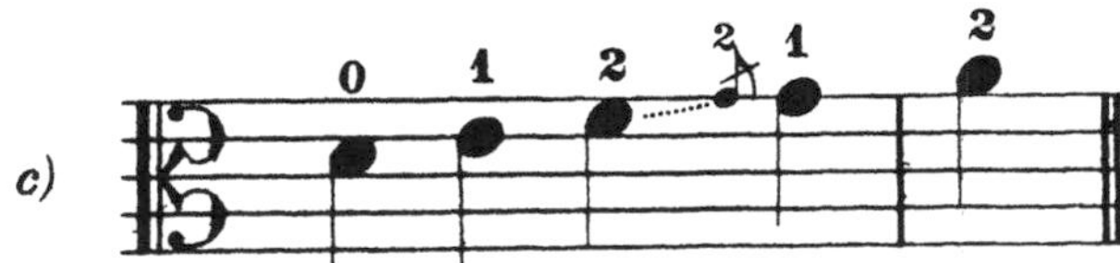

Important Rule

In this type of shift either ascending or descending, THE FIRST FINGER MUST NEVER LEAVE THE STRING.

In example *c)* **ascending,** the first and second fingers make the glide. At the instant the first finger reaches the new position the second finger is raised.

In example *d)* **descending,** the first finger starts the glide. At the instant the first finger passes the position of the next note to be sounded, that finger should fall in place. The first finger however, should continue the glide until it reaches its regular position.

Do not forget that the thumb and wrist precede the fingers in the descending shift. THIS IS IMPORTANT.

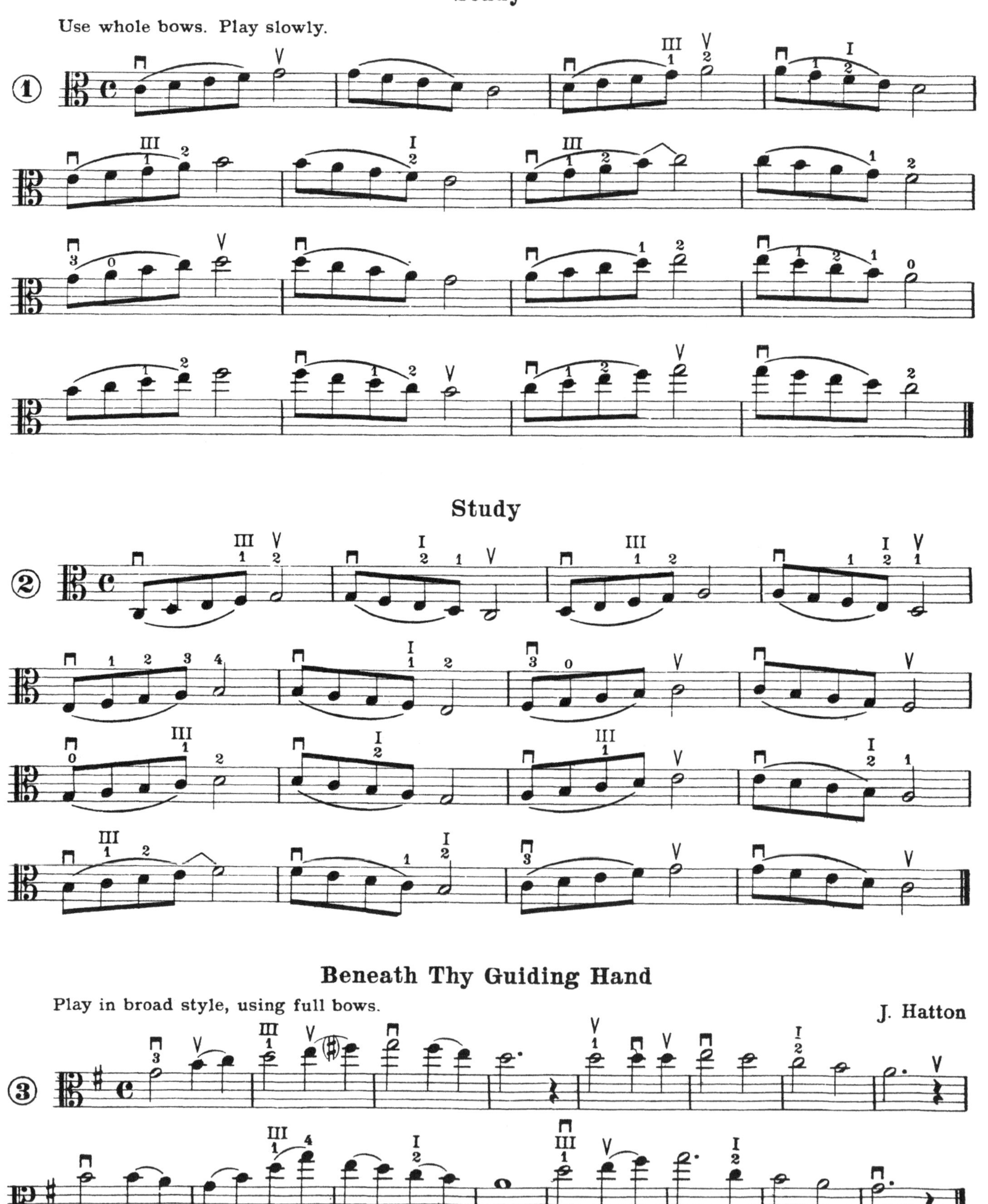
Study
Use whole bows. Play slowly.
Study
Beneath Thy Guiding Hand
Play in broad style, using full bows.
J. Hatton

Étude

Fr. Wohlfahrt, Op. 45, No. 37

Use upper half of bow. Watch intonation and rhythm.

Study

This is a study, to develop fluency in shifting. PRACTICE DAILY.

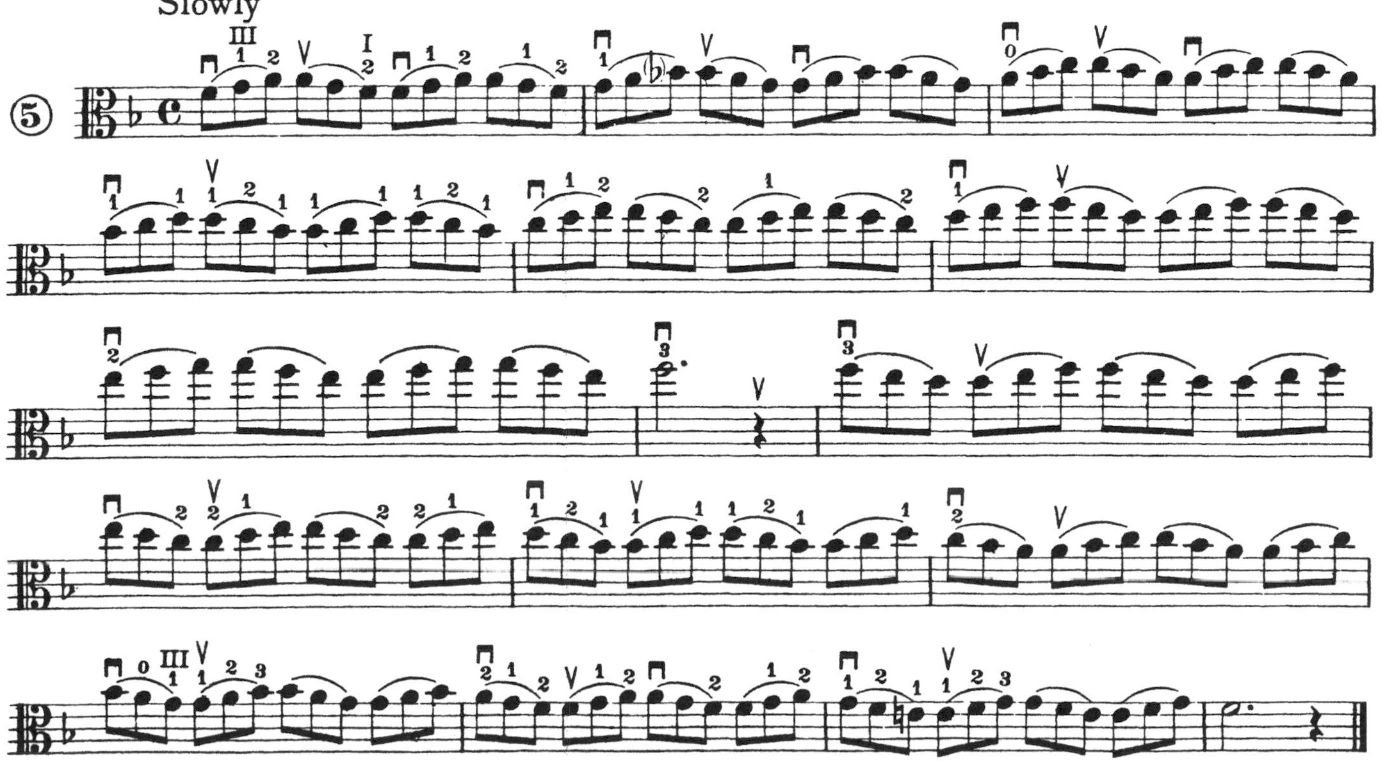

CHAPTER VII

Harmonics

Harmonics, light flute-like tones are produced by very gently touching the string at certain divisions of its length, (between the nut and bridge) such as quarter, third and half.

At this time we shall study the harmonic in the octave of the open string by dividing its length in half.

By extending the fourth finger, either a whole or half step, from the third position we arrive at the exact center of the string, at which point, by very lightly touching the string with the fleshy part of the finger tip we will sound the first harmonic of that string, one octave higher than its open tone. In playing harmonics all other fingers must be lifted.

The bow should be drawn nearer to the fingerboard and with reduced pressure upon the strings.

HARMONIC from the left *HARMONIC from the right*

Octave harmonics may also be reached from any finger in the first position. Allow the sliding finger to glide to the third position, whereupon the fourth finger, in its extended position, lightly touches the string. As the fourth finger takes its position, the other fingers must be lifted.

CHAPTER VIII

Two études for the study of substitution of fingers on the same tone. Use whole bows throughout.

CHAPTER IX

The Second Position

This position, lying midway between the first and third positions, is located by moving the first finger, thumb and hand, one note above the first position on the fingerboard.

Many passages in viola music may be played advantageously in the second position thereby avoiding the necessity of constantly shifting between the first and third positions. A thorough knowledge of the fingering for this position is quite necessary for a well-rounded viola technic.

SECOND position from the left

SECOND position from the right

F Major Scale and Arpeggio

In the Second Position

Second Position continued

Long, Long Ago

Thos. H. Bayle

B♭ Scale and Arpeggio

First and Second Positions

Deck the Hall

Old Welsh

Play with a relaxed forearm stroke, legato, without accents.

Fr. Wohlfahrt, Op. 45, No. 48

11

Play with a broad forearm stroke with a free wrist. Hold the first and fourth fingers down when stopping the octaves.

Fr. Wohlfahrt, Op. 45, No. 50

12

The Half-Position

A thorough understanding of the half-position as well as the second position (page 27) will greatly improve the smoothness and agility of your playing. The constant gliding of the first finger from the 1st position to the ½ position and back to the 1st position is not conducive to good legato playing. By the use of the half-position this gliding of the first finger backward and forward is avoided as shown in the following examples. Note the correct and incorrect fingerings.

① A B C — Correct / Incorrect

② A B C D — Correct / Incorrect

③ A B C D — Correct / Incorrect

④ ½ Pos. — I Pos. — Correct / Incorrect

⑤ ½ Pos. — I Pos. — Correct / Incorrect

⑥ ½ Pos. — I Pos. — Correct / Incorrect

Use of the half position in playing chromatic scales.

⑦

The following study in thirds illustrates the correct use of the half-position as compared to the first position (incorrect) and the second position (possible).

⑧

Technical Exercises

As an aid to truer intonation it cannot be too strongly recommended that the student devote a part of his daily practice period to the following exercises. They should be played slowly, at first gradually increasing the speed. Give special attention to the development of a keen sense of relative pitch in hearing the various intervals.

DEVELOP THE HABIT OF LISTENING MORE CRITICALLY TO YOUR OWN PLAYING.

* Hold fingers down

Half Step between 2nd and 3rd Fingers

Half Step between 1st and 2nd Fingers

Half Step between Open String and 1st Finger

Half Step between 3rd and 4th Fingers

Various Combinations of Intervals

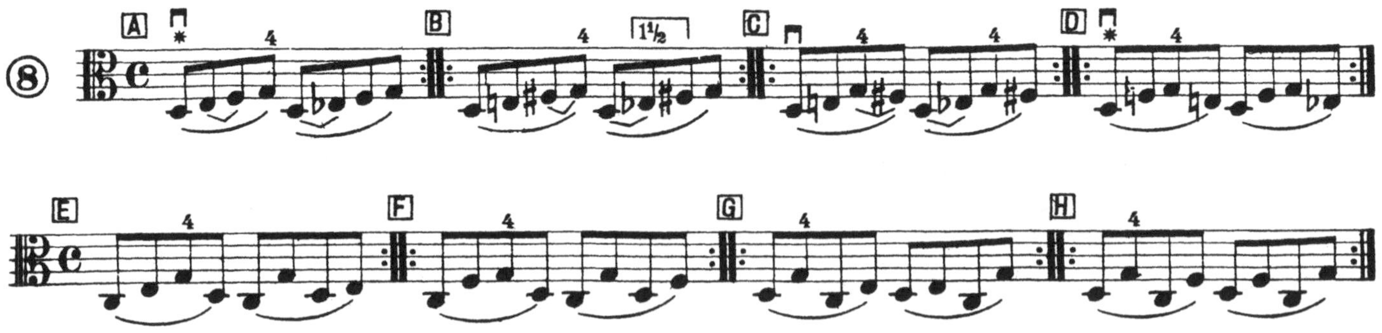

Practise the above exercises on different strings.